Fingering Chart: Oboe (Cont.)

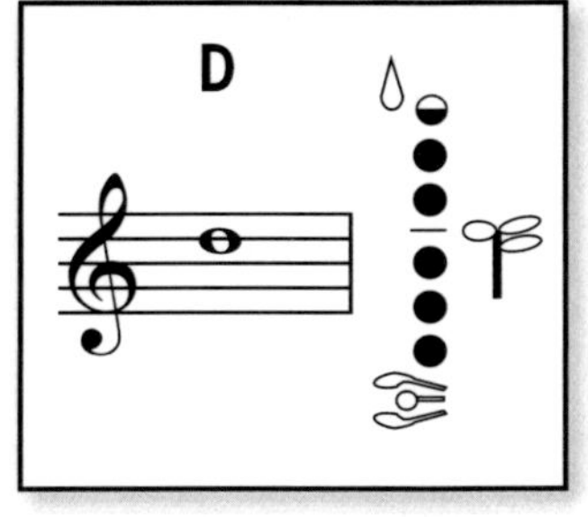

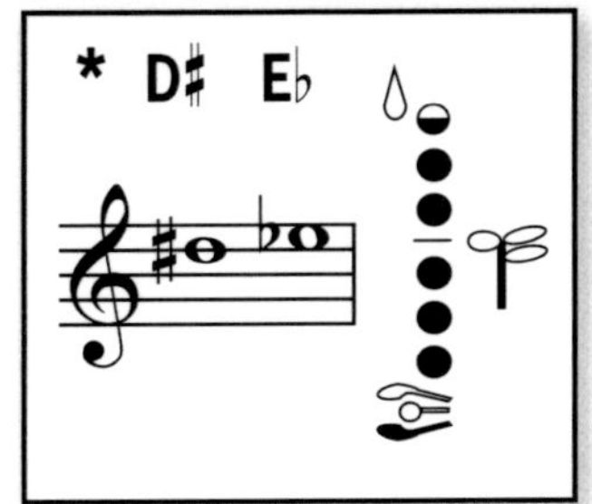

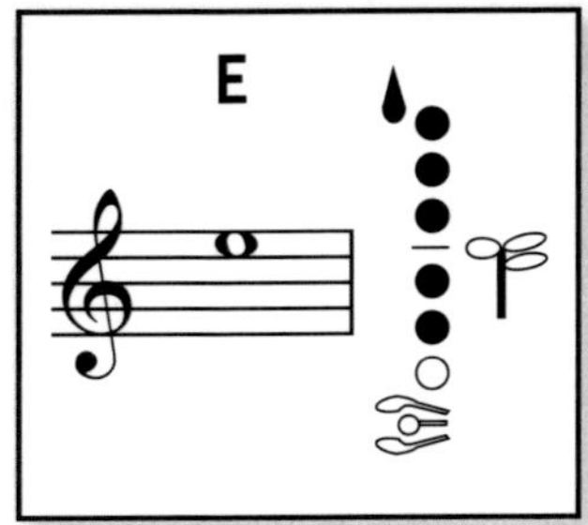

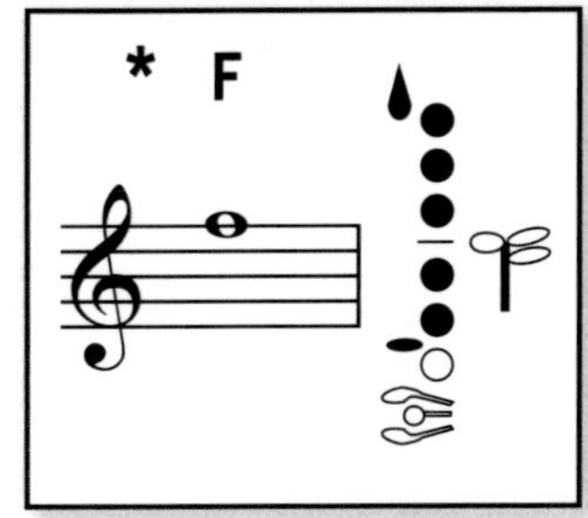

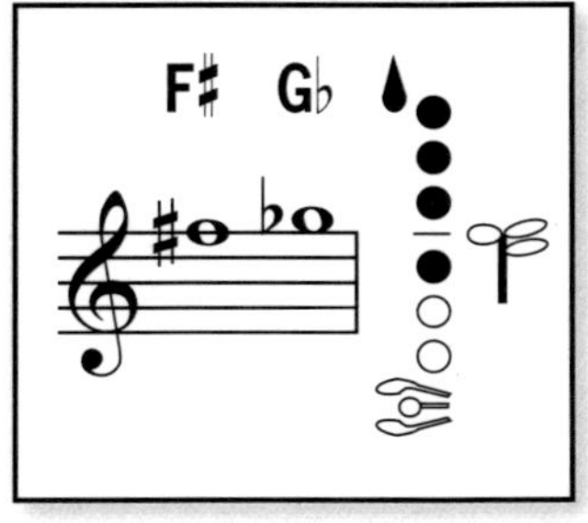

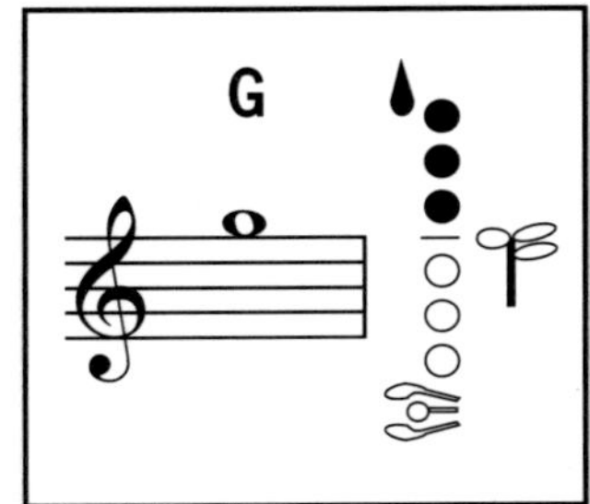

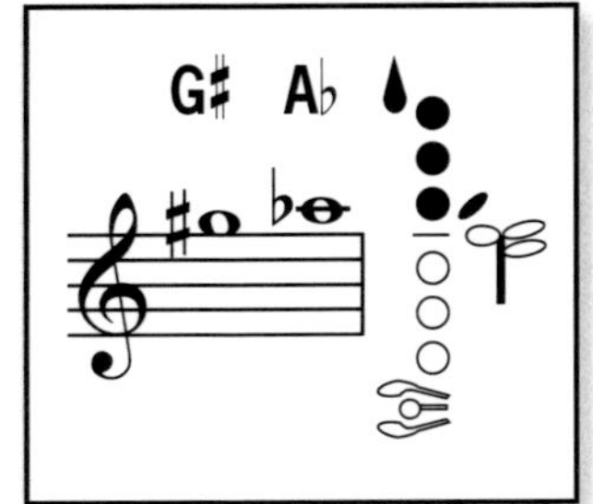

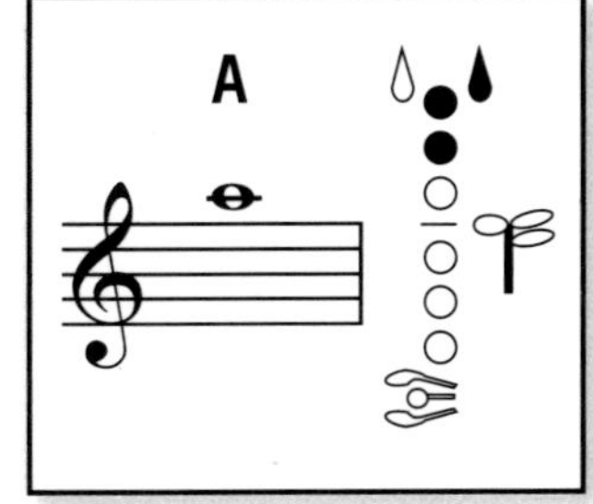

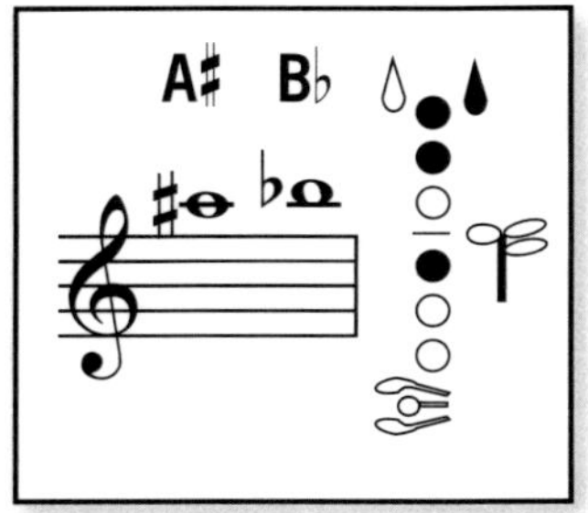

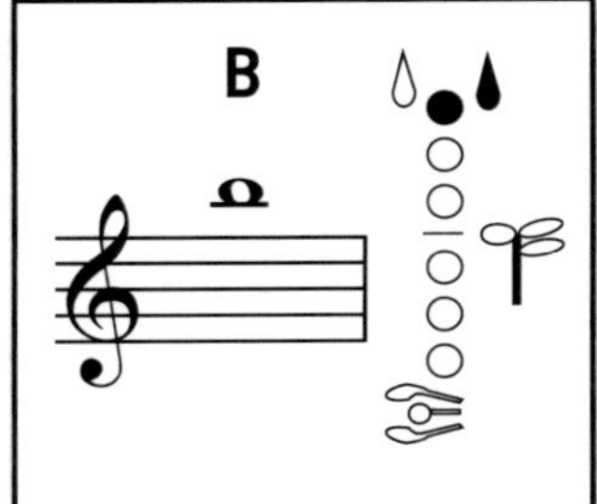

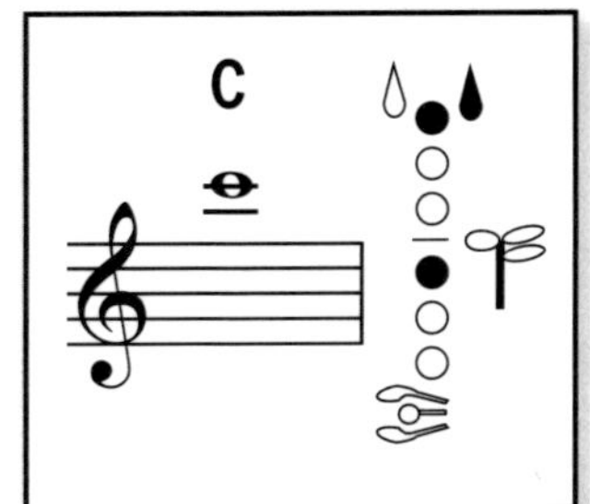

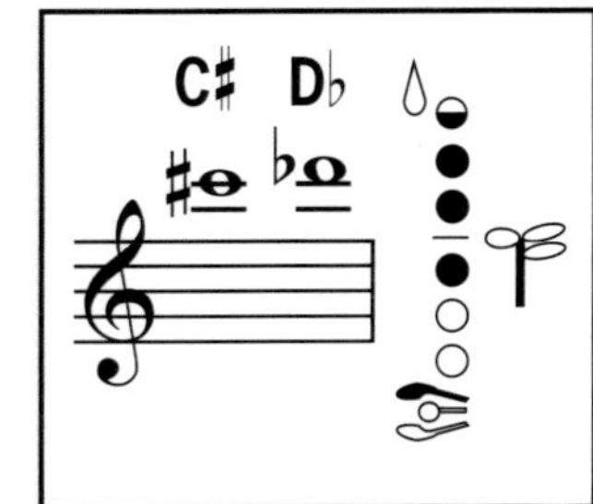

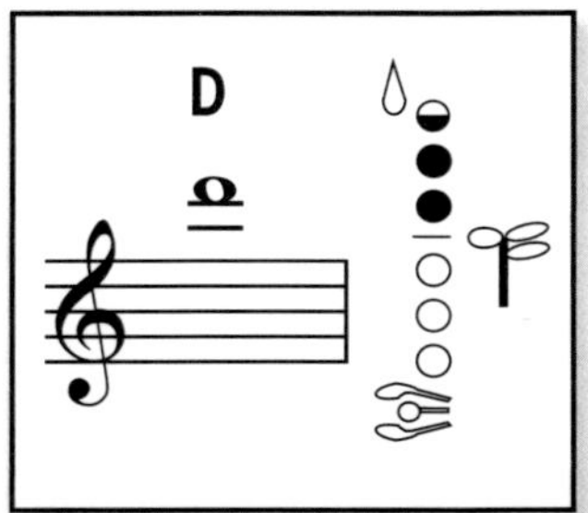

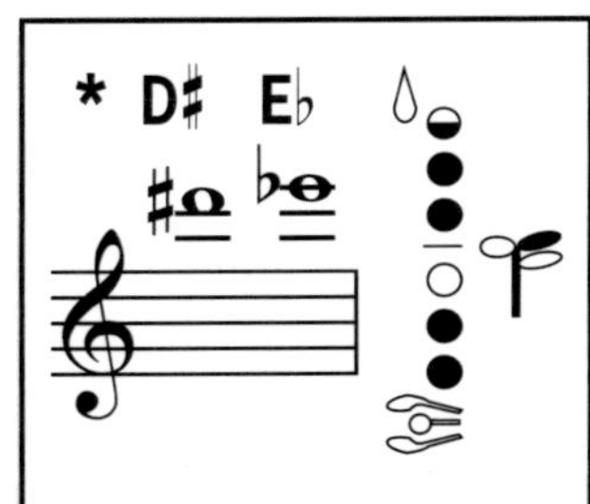

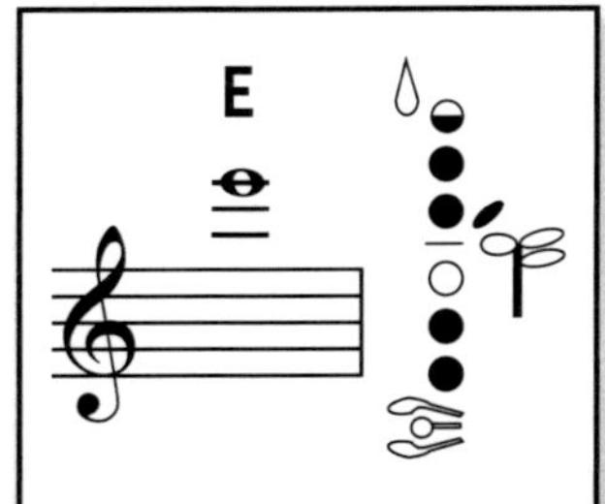

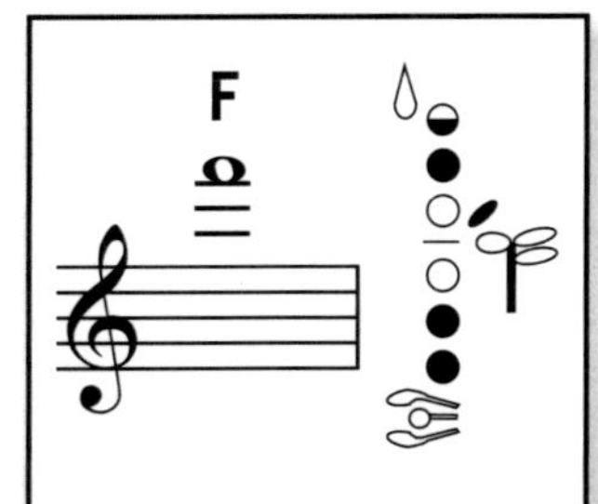

*Common Alternate Fingering Chart

Alternate fingerings are used to make some note patterns smoother. These patterns are found in the scales and arpeggios on the back of this chart.

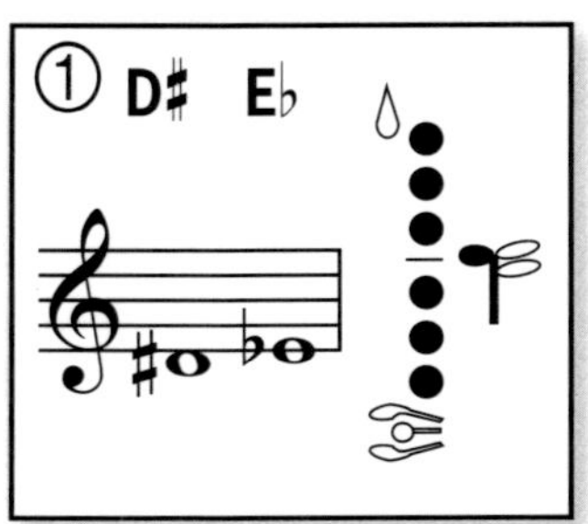

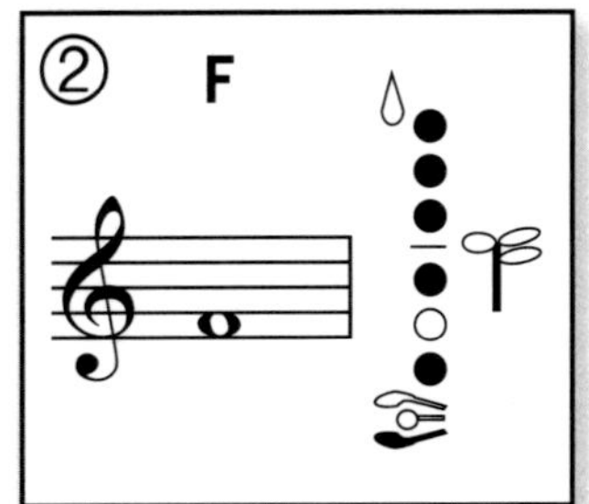

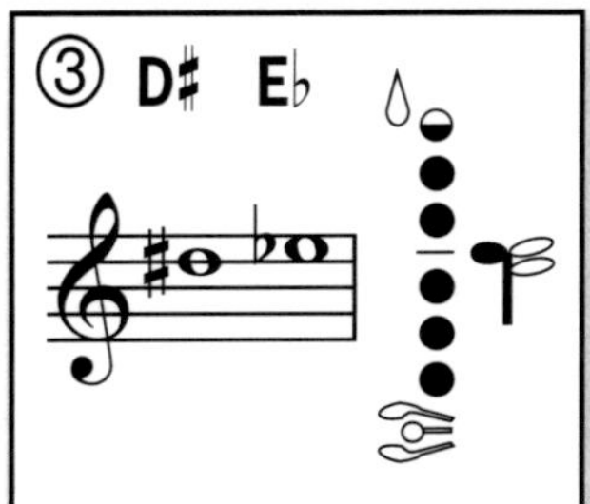

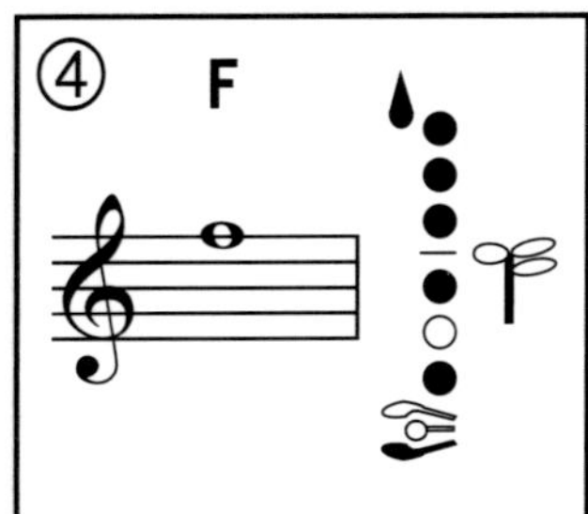

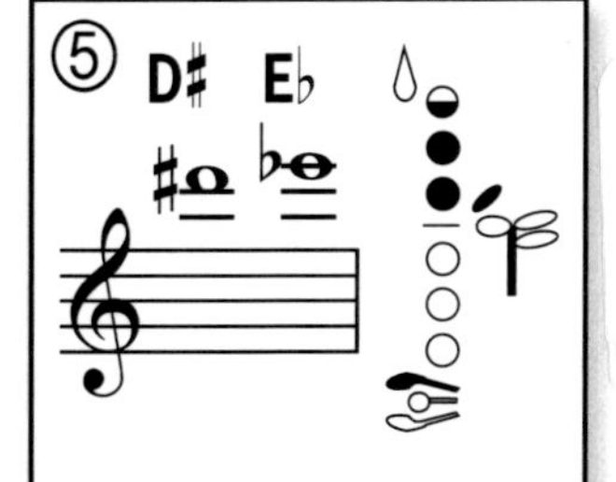

Major Scales and Arpeggios

Key of B♭

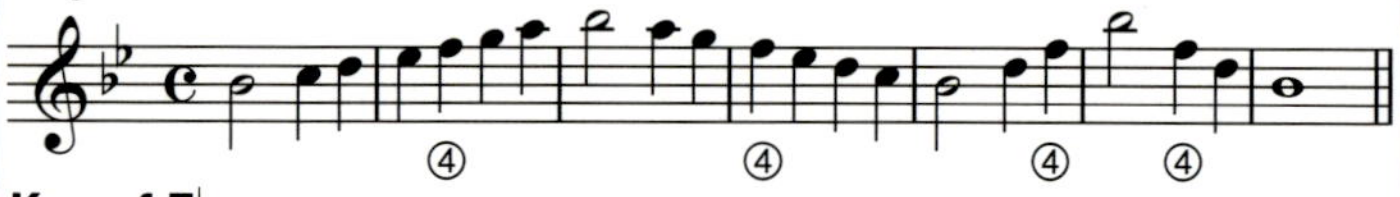

Key of E♭

Key of A♭

Key of D♭

Key of G♭

Key of B

Key of F

Key of C

Key of G

Key of D

Key of A

Key of E

Minor Scales (Harmonic Mode) and Arpeggios

Key of G minor

Key of C minor

Key of F minor

Key of B♭ minor

Key of E♭ minor

Key of A♭ minor

Key of D minor

Key of A minor

Key of E minor

Key of B minor

Key of F♯ minor

Key of C♯ minor

Chromatic Scale

The circled number below a note refers to the recommended alternate fingering (see *Common Alternate Fingering* chart).

$9.99

ISBN 978-078-667-573-9

MB20398

$9.99 USD